T0196221

Lord,
None of This
Makes Any Sense

Shirley Davis

authorHOUSE®

AuthorHouse™
1663 Liberty Drive
Bloomington, IN 47403
www.authorhouse.com
Phone: 1 (800) 839-8640

Published by AuthorHouse 01/25/2017

ISBN: 978-1-5246-6001-7 (sc)
ISBN: 978-1-5246-6002-4 (e)

Library of Congress Control Number: 2017900685

Print information available on the last page.

Discord

The preacher asked the question "what is in your house"?
I thought about it for a while before I opened my mouth,
I wanted to say "come an see everything is lovely".
But I knew in my heart that would **not** be a true story.
I would be lieing perpetration a fraud–because if the truth
be told my house is in **DISCORD.**
Constant dispute and regret even though I try to do my
very best!
It seems to me it gets worse all mixed up and chaos like a
full **purse.**
For a while I think I see the light and I start to HOPE!
But it start to slip like a bar of soap.
How did it get this way?
What brought it to this point?
Will it get better and when will it happen?
How did home, church and God's word turn into discord?
Peace turned into arguments, strife and conflict and the
whole nine yards.
The only way to end discord is to cast your cares and depend
on **GOD!**

Life Ain't Living

Hello. HELLO. Are you there? Can you hear me?
Are you alive? Well--- are you?
What makes you alive? Breathing, your
heart pumping, then what?
Are you living? What is living? Do you
have a life?
Realize who you are—"to yourself be true."
You go to sleep, wake up, go to work and come home.
Then you sit **in your big chair** and say
to yourself "**this is the life**".
Wait--- is living having a home, kids or a wife?
How do you define life? Can you hear, see, and think?
If you stop breathing, can't think or move, are you alive?
If all your senses stop --all five!
Are you happy and have something to live for?
You were born with a purpose. Then
what is your purpose?
You are a unique pattern –totally original!
May the work you have done speak for you?
Our rights are for **life, liberty and
the pursuit of happiness**.
Is life simple existence---I exist therefore I live.
Really? Who would have thunk?
God gave you life and he designed a plan—.
HELP SOMEBODY SO YOUR
LIVING WONT BE IN VAIN!
I HOPE THIS POEM CAUSED
YOUR LIFE TO CHANGE!

No one cares

Look around you —can you see no one cares.
THOES THAT SAY I LOVE YOU LOVE YOU WITH RESTRICTION,
THEY LOVE YOU ON THE SURFACE.
TO GO DEEPER REQUIRES TOO MUCH TIME AND EFFORT.
BUT I AIN'T MAD AT YOU. BECAUSE THE PERSON YOU ARE
CONNECTED TO DON'T HAVE A CLUE.
YOU CRY YOURSELF TO SLEEP AT NIGHT. IT SEEM YOUR
HORMONES HAVE YOU UPTIGHT.
YOUR FAMILY ASK THE QUESTION "HOW ARE YOU" BUT DO THEY
REALLY WANT TO KNOW.
THERE ACTIONS AND WHAT THEY DO SURE DOESN'T SHOW.
THEY SEEM TO ACT LIKE THEY DON'T CARE. BUT THEY HAVE
BURDENS THAT THEY HAVE TO BEAR.
PEOPLE MOVE AROUND IN THE HOUSE BUT THEY DON'T SEE
EACH OTHER.
HOW LONG WILL IT TAKE TO SEE I HAVE NO COVE?
WOULD IT MATTER OR MAKE A DIFFERENCE TO YOU IF I
DISAPPEAR. OR WOULD LIFE GO ON AS USUAL AS IF I AM HERE.
MANY WOULD GIVE YOU FLOWERS WHEN YOU DIE. BUT I PREFER
MY BOUQUET WHILE I AM ALIVE.
WHEN YOU ARE DEAD YOU CAN'T SMELL YOU ARE DEAD.
DEAD- DEAD- DEAD SO THERE IS NOTHING ELSE TO BE SAID!!!

The Skin I'm In

Hello! Can you see me!

Wait let me undress-- NO wait let me take off my skin.

Now can you see me, do you know who I am?

A mother, a woman, a wife,

Struggling for the rest of my life.

You see what you want to see, **but- is- it- really me?**

I work from day to day.

For minimal wage and minimal pay.

The skin I'm in, I must always wear.

But it would be nice if we could share.

It gets tight sometime and I WANT OUT!

BUT IT DOESN'T CHANGE AS
MUCH AS I SHOUT.

We are different that is what makes us unique.

Not our body size or our physique

So I stand tall and do what I do.

Accept what I can't change and **you should too!**

Lord None Of This Makes Any Sense

I ASKED THE LORD THE OTHER DAY
"PLEASE DON'T KEEP ME IN SUSPENSE".
WHAT IS GOING ON IN OUR WORLD
NONE OF THIS MAKES ANY SENSE.
FAMILIES ARE JOINED TOGETHER
ONLY WITH THEIR BLOOD.
BUT FAMILIES ARE DYSFUNCTIONAL
EVERY SINCE NOAH AND THE FLOOD.
LIVING IN THE SAME HOUSE FATHERS
AND MOTHERS DON'T HAVE A CLUE.
THE NEIGHBORS KNOW MORE ABOUT
YOUR CHILDREN THAN YOU DO.
"CAN YOU FEEL ME" IS THE
SLOGAN OF THE DAY.
WELL IT'S HARD TO FEEL YOU WE
HAVEN'T TALKED SENSE LAST MAY.
IN MY HOUSE WITH MY CHILDREN 24-7
RAISING THEM FOR MANY YEARS.
BUT THEY ARE MORE INFLUNCED
BY THEIR PEERS.
WATCHING PEOPLE, I WONDER
DO ANY OF US CONNECT?
IS IT A MIRAGE, A LIFE FILLED WITH REGRET?
SISTERS AND BROTHERS LIVING IN THE SAME
HOUSE HAVE A DIFFERENT POINT OF VIEW.
JUST LIKE MEMBERS OF THE SAME CHURCH
SITTING ON A DIFFERENT PEW.
YOU KNOW LORD--- WHAT CAN I DO? THINGS
GET SO MIXED UP **IT'S HARD TO SEE YOU.**

Sixty

SIXTY SIXTY THATS NOT ME --I
WAS JUST FIFTEEN YOU SEE.
I DREAMED OF THE DAYS WHEN I WOULD
BE GROWN, TALKED AND TALKED ABOUT
REAPING WHAT I HAD HAVE SOWN.
LOOKED FORWARD TO THE TIME WHEN
I COULD MAKE MY OWN DECISIONS.
BUT DIDN'T UNDERSTAND THE DECISION
WOULD HAVE A CONCLUSION.
IT TOOK A LONG TIME BUT
LIFE BEGIN TO HAPPEN
IT TWISTED AND TURNED
UNTIL I BECAME DIZZY,
TRYING TO DEAL AND KEEP MYSELF BUSY.
WHAT HAPPENED I TRIED
TO FIGURE IT OUT!
ACTED LIKE A LITTLE GIRL
AND BEGIN TO POUT.
BUT IT DID NOT SOLVE THE PROBLEMS---
THEY DID NOT GO AWAY.
WITH ALL YOUR SITUATIONS
THERE IS A PRICE TO PAY.
LIFE HAVE A WAY OF SNEAKING UP ON YOU.
IT'S CAUSED BY THE THINGS YOU DO.
20-30-40-50- AND SIXTY
WHERE DID YOU GO.
SOME YEARS MOVED FAST
AND SOME MOVED SLOW.

YOU HOPE THAT IT IS NOT IN
VAIN—BECAUSE OF ALL THE
HEARTACHE AND PAIN!
OKAY SIXTY BRING IT ON---
BUT YOU FORGOT I WILL REAP
<u>EVERYTHING</u> I HAVE SOWN.

Life Is Short

Life is short —so don't take it for granted.
Walking around as though you are permanently planted.
Don't concentrate on the little things like this and that.
Paying more attention to your dog and your cat!
What's important you choose to ignore!
But idle gossip you always want more.
Girl what's the latest? Tell me the news.
Don't you know you have a destiny to choose?
Go ahead do what you want to do.
But one day death will come for you!
What will you say "I'm not ready --come
back tomorrow night".
There are a few things I must make right.
Live everyday like it is your last!
Try to correct anything you can from your past.
LIFE IS SHORT—NO MATTER
HOW MANY YEARS!
We all must experience joy and some tears.
Will the work you have done speak well of you.
YOU WILL REAP WHAT YOU HAVE
SOWN BEFORE YOU ARE THROUGH!

Something Is Wrong

The churches were filled this morning
for many given reasons.
Some came to give God praise and others for the season.
Well the day has gone and night far spent.
Are you much better for the time you went?
Week after week-- year after year
What do you do when all the people disappear?
Does anything change or do things remain the same.
What are we doing playing some kind of game?
Churches on every corner, what does the name mean?
A tabernacle, a temple, a synagogue--
choose your place of worship.
How do you baptize a sprinkle or a dip?
Is it relative? Does it cause a change?
Is it done in Jesus name?
You come you go, continue with the tradition.
We will continue to do the same. We
refuse to change our position.
Did you know insanity is doing the same thing,
and expecting a different result.
There must be a change because something is wrong.
Change the hymn and sing a new song.
Christians go to church—sinners pass bye.
No one questions or ask the reason why.
We just accept the status quo,
Like a day we come and go.
Something is wrong, you may agree--
don't do anything and you will see.

Talking -PLEASE SHUT UP

We talk to people all day long-- people we don't know--
people we don't want to talk to-- but it is what is expected
of us. Don't be rude-- be polite. What if I don't feel like
talking. The question always comes up "why aren't you
saying anything--" Don't you hear me?" Answer me!
No I won't-- I am tired—tried of constantly
talking and saying "nothing."
Shut up be quiet-- you have nothing to say. Study to be
Quiet. If your talking isn't an improvement to silence,
be quiet. Half of what you say is not important anyway.
Foolish idle conversation that we won't remember
past today. Talking to be seen or heard is not worth
it. If I can just find the right words. LORD tell me
what to say-- tell me what you want me to do.
HIS ANSWER--"Let the words of YOUR mouth and
the meditation of YOUR heart be acceptable in MY site"

What Do You See

When you LOOK AT me what do you see-- a fool, a joke
a nincompoop
someone to laugh at- make fun of—she doesn't matter-- she's
not important, irrelevant. Why should I care what she thinks
or feel? Walk by-- don't take the time. make excuses-- (I
need to take a nap, wash my hair, look at my program on
TV), it requires too much effort

But when **you** are in trouble **everybody should pay
attention.** Make **you** their top priority. Focus-focus on
me I'm over here-- crowd around.

It's all about **me**-- I should monopolize your time and all
your effort.

What can **you** see now—are things different can **you**
empathize?

COULD **YOU** APOLOGIZE OR SYMPATHIZE.

Take a second look then you would rewrite the book.

Life is a give and take—sometimes you are **asleep** and
sometimes you are **awake**.

**Seeing is not always believing it is the way you
interpret things.**

Help us to be alert--- to hear when the bell rings.

Look beyond yourself –NOW what do you see?

A different picture of what GOD has for you and ME!!

Life Ain't Living

Hello. HELLO. Are you there? Can you hear me?
Are you alive? Well--- are you?
What makes you alive? Breathing, your
heart pumping, then what?
Are you living? What is living? Do you have a life?
Realize who you are—"to yourself be true."
You go to sleep, wake up, go to work and come home.
Then you sit **in your big chair** and say
to yourself "**this is the life**".
Wait--- is living having a home, kids or a wife?
How do you define life? Can you hear, see, and think?
If you stop breathing, can't think or move, are you alive?
If all your senses stop --all five!
Are you happy and have something to live for?
You were born with a purpose. Then
what is your purpose?
You are a unique pattern –totally original!
May the work you have done speak for you?
Our rights are for **life, liberty and
the pursuit of happiness**.
Is life simple existence---I exist therefore I live.
Really? Who would have thunk?
God gave you life and he designed a plan—.
HELP SOMEBODY SO YOUR
LIVING WONT BE IN VAIN!
I HOPE THIS POEM CAUSED
YOUR LIFE TO CHANGE!

Written by Shirley P. Davis

Wandering

Wandering around in the maze of life going nowhere quickly.

From "this" to "that" trying to get from 'here" to "there".

If only we could give our mind a rest.

Cut down the confusion and reduce some of the stress.

Things would be clearer if we exam our selves in the mirror.

We look at life with a distorted view.

Who want to go though life looking just like YOU!

I will do this but I won't do that.

You kill my dog I will kill your cat.

Wandering don't always have to be bad—it makes you think about the good things you had.

Look at your life −can you figure it out? If you can give us a shout.

We want to celebrate you, so we can figure it out too.

Don't give up,we must keep trying, working until the bell toll for the dying.

Let's find something to do to occupy our time.

WRITE A GOOD POEM OR MAKE UP A GOOD RHYME!

What If...

WHAT IF IT WERE YOU-- LONELY, SCARED
AND DON'T KNOW WHAT TO DO.
YOU LIFE IN CHAOS ---YOUR
DREAMS AND HOPE LOST.
WHAT IF IT WERE YOU SEARCHING FOR A
PURPOSE IN LIFE, TRYING TO SOLVE YOUR
PROBLEMS WITH A GUN OR A KNIFE?
WHAT IF IT WERE YOU THAT WAS TOLD
"YOU WILL NEVER BE ANYTHING".
BUT YOU WANT TO FIT IN WITH
THE HOMMIES AND HANG.
WHAT IF IT WERE YOU WHO MADE
A MISTAKE –SHOOK UP THE WORLD
AND CAUSE AN EARTHQUAKE?
WHAT IF THEY TOLD YOU WERE "SLOW"
AND GAVE NO OPTION –NO PLACE TO GO!
WHAT IF IT WERE YOU --TRAPPED IN
STATISTICS AND CIRCUMSTANCES?
NO TIME TO CHOOSE WITH
WHOM YOU CAN DANCE.
What if it WERE you born with three strikes against you?
You have to make a choice, what are you GONNA do.
IS THERE ANYONE THAT I CAN DEPEND?
HELP ME SURVIVE AND HELP ME TO
TO WIN.
WHAT IF THERE WAS A SAVIOR
WHO COULD GIVE YOU LIFE.
WOULD YOU FORGIVE AND
GIVE UP YOUR STRIVE?

WE ALL HAVE A BASIC NEED
TO BE **LOVED** and FIT IN
BE accepted and cared for by a dear friend.
But if you take the time to empathize,
You would be helpful and considered very wise.
WRITTEN BY SHIRLEY P. DAVIS

Words

PEOPLE TALKING EVERYWHERE-
ON THE PHONE, TELEVISION,
AND TO EACH OTHER ETC.
BUT IS THERE ANY
COMMUNICATION GOING ON?
TO TALK IS TO SPEAK WORDS, TO
COMMUNICATE IS TO EXCHANGE A
THOUGHT IDEA OR IMPRESSION.
NEGATIVE WORDS OR POSITIVE
WORDS- -THEY ARE JUST- -
WORDS DO THEY HAVE
ANY MEANING --=I HOPE SO.
MY WORDS ON THIS PAPER WILL
THEY BE REMEMBERED WILL
THEY CAUSE YOU TO THINK?
I DO HAVE SOMETHING TO SHARE AND SO DO
YOU. BUT DO YOU CARE? ARE WE OCCUPYING
TIME AND SPACE? OR WE SHARING A PART
OF OURSELVES OR JUST MERE WORDS.
REMEMBERED NOW- - WORDS ARE
ONLY A PART OF THE ALPHABET.
THE LETTERS REARRANGED IN
SOME TYPE OF ORDER.
STIMULATE MY MIND-ENCOURAGE
MY SPIRIT- TOUCH MY HEART.
MAKE ME KNOW I AM ALIVE AND NOT
JUST GOING THOUGH THE MOTIONS.
I WANT

TO BE HEARD AND NOT NECESSARILY SEEN.
SO I HOPE MY STORY IS CLEARLY TOLD. YOU
TELL ME IF I HAVE ACCOMPLISHED MY GOAL

SHIRLEY P. DAVIS

Trust

Looking at nothing believing on something.

Lord I trust you.

Forgetting the things that are behind and pressing for the mark of the high calling.

Lord I trust you.

Perplexed on every side, persecuted and not destroyed

Lord I trust you.

Leaning not unto my own understanding but always acknowledging you.

Lord I trust you.

For the blessing of the Lord maketh one rich and added no sorry.

Lord I trust you.

Hoping against hope and then going beyond.

Lord I trust you.

Many are the afflictions of the righteous but the Lord delivers out if them all.

Lord I trust you.

Weeping may endure... but joy comes in the morning.

Lord I trust you.

Relationship

RELATIONSHIP A THING OF THE PAST.
RELATIONSHIP THEY SAY WON'T LAST. NOT
PASSION OR DESIRE. IT'S MORE THAN THE
CLIQUE "COME ON BABY LIGHT MY FIRE".
WILL RELATIONSHIP LAST LONG
AFTER THE TRILL IS GONE.
IT IS WHAT MAKE YOU WANT TO COME HOME?
TO LOVE—ADD COMMUNICATION,
UNDERSTANDING AND A OPEN MIND.
YOU WILL NEED THIS WITH
RELATIONSHIP ALL THE TIME.
EMPATHY HELPS YOU PUT
YOURSELF IN MY PLACE.
SHOW SOME KINDNESS, MERCY
AND A WHOLE LOT OF GRACE.
COMMUNICATION IS ESSENTIAL
TO THIS WHOLE IDEA.
IT CLARIFIES THE PICTURE AND
MAKES EVERYTHING CLEAR.
LOVE COVERS A MULTITUDE OF THINGS.
EVEN AFTER THE FAT LADY SINGS.
OVER THE YEARS I HAVE COME TO
KNOW, WHAT BUILDS A RELATIONSHIP
AND HOW IT GROWS.
IF YOU PUT SOME EFFORT IT WILL SHOW.
LEARN FROM EXPERIENCE IT
IS THE BEST TEACHER.
FOR PAIN, HURTS AND DISAPPOINTMENTS
ARE NOT A NICE PREACHER.

RELATIONSHIPS DEVELOP FOR A
PURPOSE AND A REASON.
YOUR GIFT IS YOU AND IT'S
PERFECT FOR ANY SEASON.

Sadness

Sadness comes from within if you open up and let it in.

But the sadness thing of all is no one to pick you up when you fall?

You sit in a crowded room but you are alone. Let me tell you to go to the throne.

I recommend someone to talk to, who time after time has brought you though.

He sticketh closer than a brother and helps you go a little further.

Sadness seeks to return again and again, but before the process begin, let me introduce you to my friend.

He died so you can have life and reduce all you fear and strife.

Some People—
Written For Denzel Davis

Some people seek for life--not me I seek for hope and peace.
For what is life --without peace?
Like working from day to day full
time and getting no pay.
Is there a reason to be here--trying to
hold on to those we hold dear.
But inside is turmoil and pain--but I
still must **play this game.**
There is a season for life but I have
not truly found the purpose.
Maybe it's lying beneath the surface.
Some people concentrate on money and wealth!
Then they realize it doesn't matter if
you are not in good health.
You can't take back the past but you
know this too won't last.
Shedding tears wont remove the years.
Some people LIVE life only in the moment--
-always viewing others as your opponent.
They manage to get by from day to day--
that's because they listen by others hearsay.
Why do I care what other people think? Because
without them my life would be blank.
No one is an island, we intertwine in some way.
We cross each other's path from day to day.

I may have an opinion and so do you.
I may not think or believe like you do.
So, don't be the **some people** I talk about!
Life is short and there are things you can do **without!**

But It's Not Love Fault

LOVE IS NOT CHOOSY IT FALLS WHERE IT MAY.
BUT IS IT LOVES FAULT WHEN IT DECIDES NOT
TO STAY?
IT'S FUNNY YOU DON'T INVITE IT BUT IT COMES
IN IT'S OWN TIME.
YOU MIGHT SAY IT HAS IT'S OWN MIND.
LOVE WHY DO YOU PLAY GAMES WITH MY
SANITY?
LOVE SOMETIMES MAKES IT HARD FOR ME
TO SEE.

SOME TIMES I WISH YOU NEVER CAME.
THEN IT WOULD NOT BE NECESSARY TO PLAY
THIS GAME.
REFLECTING ON WHAT USED TO BE,HOW GREAT
AND WONDERFUL IT WAS JUST YOU AND ME.
BUT REALITY HAS SET IN,FOR THIS IS A GAME I
MIGHT NOT WIN.

An Oak Tree

Like an oak tree you stood the test of time.
Bending and swaying from time to time.
The winds blew and storms came, but you were steadfast
and remained the same!
I marvel at your strength and courage.
Always taking your time, there seemed to be no hurray.
Never complained-you said there was no need.
So patience is planted like a seed.
Your strength gave me courage to go another mile.
Just looking at you made me smile!
I know many times you felt like giving up, Lord help me
bare this bitter cup.
Your branches were built with love and covered a multitude
of sins.
Holding no hate or jealousy within.
Knowing you have blessed my life and It shall
Made me a better mother, Christian and wife.
SLEEP MOM FOR YOU DESERVE YOUR REST
FOR YOU HAVE BEEN STRONG AND PAST THE
TEST!

The Ostrich Affect

BURY YOU HEAD AND IT WILL GO
AWAY—IT'S THE OSTRICH AFFECT.
DON'T DARE LOOK AT IT, ADMIT
IT OR ADDRESS IT,
USE THE OSTRICH AFFECT. WHY
STRESS, TEST, OR GET INVOLVED
IN THE MESS USE THE OSTRICH AFFECT.
WILL IT SOLVE YOUR PROBLEMS
OR MAKE THEM GO AWAY,
PROBABLY NOT FOR THEY ARE HERE TO STAY.
TROUBLE GOES DOWN AN ALLEY
OR STREET THEN IT GOES HOME
WITH WHOMEVER HE MEET.
BURYING YOUR HEAD DOESN'T WORK
ANYWAY, IT POST PONE YOUR DESTINY
AND YOUR SOLUTIONS DELAY.
GIVE IT A TRY IT MIGHT FOR A WHILE, IT
MIGHT EVEN MAKE SOMEONE SMILE.
PULL THE COVERS OVER YOUR HEAD
AND YOUR FEET WILL STICK OUT.
IGNORE YOU PROBLEMS OR
JUST SIT AND POUT.
DON'T ANSWER THE PHONE,
MAKE AN EXCUSE AND JUST STAY AT HOME.
USE THE OSTRICH AFFECT. BUT THE
OSTRICH WILL MINIMIZE YOUR PROGRESS
AND DECREASE YOU EFFECTIVENESS.
YOU CAN CONTINUE TO PLAY THE
GAME-- BUT IT WONT SOLVE ANYTHING
OR BRING ABOUT A CHANGE.

Lord None Of This Makes Any Sense?

I asked the Lord the other day "please don't keep in suspense. What is going on in our world none of this makes any sense."

Families joined together only by blood but families are still dysfunctional since Noah and the flood.

Living in the same house fathers and mothers don't have a clue.

Sometimes your neighbors know more about your children than you do.

"Can you feel me is the slogan off the day".

Well it's hard to understand because we haven't talked since last may.

Heads hell down focused on a phone—everywhere you look like a clone.

In my house with my family 24-7,trying to teach them for many years.

I still don't know why they will listen more to their peers.

Watching people, I wonder do any of us connect.

Or is it a mirage a faust, filled with regret.

Sisters and brothers living in the same house, have a different point of view. Just like members of the same congregation sitting on the same pew.

I try to do things God's way hoping to make a change.

In my flesh I'm losing the battle things remain the same.

Lord none of this makes no sense—can't seem to climb the fence.

sleep is turmoil twisting and turning at night.

But anytime during the day it's alright.

Is there a conclusion,is there an end.

I have to ask the question,when Lord WHEN?

Thoughts

So many thoughts going though my head,

I almost for--got what your word said---

I will prepare a table before thee --in the presence of your e-n-e my.

Let this mind be in you that was in Christ Jesus—look at ourselves as Jesus sees us.

The very gates of hell --- against his promises Satan can't prevail.

God gave us **love, power and a sound mind**----can't go by what I see or hear,

I must trust in the Lord and only him I will fear.

Weeping may endure for a night—but joy comes in the morning light.

My Daughter

My daughter gave me this computer with much love--
God you sent her- a gift from above.
She gives and gives, I guess she got that
from her mom—grand mom.
Always trying to do good—rather than **do harm**.
WHO AM I THAT THY ARE MINDFUL OF ME.
Through my daughter you let me
see- life in a positive way.
Your will and destiny she must obey.
I want to guide her to do things GOD's way.
There is a reason for everything you do.
SHEPHANIE it does not matter you have to
be you—**but** no one can do what you do.
She is not perfect for I am not naïve—but
she tries to fulfill what I perceive.
<u>GOD help me to help her fill her potential and her destiny.</u>
<u>For I see her as you do—anointed and talented</u>
<u>and I know</u> **she loves you too!**
I thank you for who you sent me because ONLY
YOU KNEW WHAT SHE WOULD BE!
Before she was born YOU KNEW HER AND
IT WAS MARVELOUS in your eyes.
I will always love her until the day she dies!

Words

PEOPLE TALKING EVERYWHERE-
ON THE PHONE, TELEVISION,
AND TO EACH OTHER ETC.
BUT IS THERE ANY
COMMUNICATION GOING ON?
TO TALK IS TO SPEAK WORDS, TO
COMMUNICATE IS TO EXCHANGE A
THOUGHT IDEA OR IMPRESSION.
NEGATIVE WORDS OR POSITIVE
WORDS- -THEY ARE JUST- -
WORDS DO THEY HAVE
ANY MEANING --=I HOPE SO.
MY WORDS ON THIS PAPER WILL
THEY BE REMEMBERED WILL
THEY CAUSE YOU TO THINK?
I DO HAVE SOMETHING TO SHARE AND SO DO
YOU. BUT DO YOU CARE? ARE WE OCCUPYING
TIME AND SPACE? OR WE SHARING A PART
OF OURSELVES OR JUST MERE WORDS.
REMEMBERED NOW- - WORDS ARE
ONLY A PART OF THE ALPHABET.
THE LETTERS REARRANGED IN
SOME TYPE OF ORDER.
STIMULATE MY MIND-ENCOURAGE
MY SPIRIT- TOUCH MY HEART.
MAKE ME KNOW I AM ALIVE AND NOT
JUST GOING THOUGH THE MOTIONS.
I WANT

TO BE HEARD AND NOT NECESSARILY SEEN.
SO I HOPE MY STORY IS CLEARLY TOLD. YOU
TELL ME IF I HAVE ACCOMPLISHED MY GOAL

SHIRLEY P. DAVIS

Printed in the United States
By Bookmasters